GREEK

Made Nice & Easy!™

Staff of Research & Education Association
Carl Fuchs, Language Program Director

Based on Language Courses developed by the U.S. Government for Foreign Service Personnel

Research & Education Association
61 Ethel Road West
Piscataway, New Jersey 08854

Dr. M. Fogiel, Director

GREEK MADE NICE & EASY™

Printed in the United States of America

Library of Congress Control Number 00-193026

International Standard Book Number 0-87891-370-X

I-1

What This Guide Will Do For You

Whether travelling to a foreign country or to your favorite international restaurant, this *Nice & Easy* guide gives you just enough of the language to get around and be understood. Much of the material in this book was developed for government personnel who are often assigned to a foreign country on a moment's notice and need a quick introduction to the language.

In this handy and compact guide, you will find useful words and phrases, popular expressions, common greetings, and the words for numbers, money, and time. Every word or phrase is accompanied with the correct pronunciation. There is a vocabulary list for finding words quickly.

Generous margins on the pages allow you to make notes and remarks that you may find helpful.

If you expect to travel to Greece, the section on the country's history and relevant up-to-date facts will make your trip more informative and enjoyable. By keeping this guide with you, you'll be well prepared to understand as well as converse in Greek.

Carl Fuchs
Language Program Director

Contents

Greek Facts and History v

Hints on Pronunciation 3

Special Points 4

Useful Words and Phrases 5

Greetings and General Phrases 5

Location 8

Directions 9

Numbers 9

What's This? 12

Asking For Things 12

Money 15

Time 15

Other Useful Phrases 17

Additional Expressions 19

Fill-In Sentences 21

Important Signs 31

Vocabulary List 33

GREECE

Facts & History

Official Name: Hellenic Republic

Geography
Area: 131,957 sq. km. (51,146 sq. mi.; roughly the size of Alabama).
Capital-Athens (population) greater Athens (3,096,775) municipality of Athens (748,110). *Other cities*-Thessaloniki (377,951), Piraeus (169,622), Greater Piraeus (880,529), Patras (172,763), Larissa (113,426), Iraklion (117,167).
Terrain: Mountainous interior with coastal plains; many islands.
Climate: Mediterranean; mild winter and hot, dry summer.

People
Population: 11.5 million.
Languages: Greek 99%; other 1%.
Religions: Greek Orthodox 98%, Muslim 1%, other 1%.
Education: *Years compulsory* - 9. *Literacy* - 93%.

Government

Type: Presidential parliamentary republic.
Independence: 1830.
Constitution: June 11, 1975, amended March 1986.
Branches: *Executive*— president (head of state), prime minister (head of government). *Legislative* — 300-seat unicameral Vouli (parliament). *Judicial* — Supreme Court.

Economy

GDP: $120.25 billion.
Per capita GDP: $11,305.
Natural resources: Bauxite, lignite, magnesite, oil, marble.
Agriculture (10% of GDP); Manufacturing (14% of GDP); Services (66.5% of GDP): Transportation, tourism, communications, trade, banking, public administration, defense. *Exports* - $10.5 billion: manufactured goods, food and beverages, petroleum products, cement, chemicals.

Language

The Greek language dates back at least 3,500 years, and modern Greek preserves many elements of its classical predecessor. In the 19th century, after Greece's War of Independence, an effort was made to rid the language of Turkish and Arabic words and expressions. The resulting version was considered to be closer to the classical Greek language of Homer and was called *Katharevousa*. However, *Katharevousa* was never adopted by most Greeks in daily speech. The commonly spoken language, called *Demotiki,* became the official language in 1976.

History of Greece

Greece has a history stretching back almost 4,000 years. The people of the mainland, called Hellenes, organized great naval and military expeditions and explored the Mediterranean and Black Seas, going as far as the Atlantic Ocean and the Caucasus Mountains. One of those expeditions, the siege of Troy, is narrated in the first great European literary work, Homer's *Iliad.* Numerous Greek settlements were founded throughout the Mediterranean, Asia Minor, and the coast of North Africa as a result of travels in search of new markets.

Archaic Period

The rebirth of Hellenism dates from the 8th century B.C. During the Iron Age, Greece, as a mountainous country with small, isolated valleys, had been organized into small "city-kingdoms." At the same time there was considerable cultural development marked mainly by the dissemination of the alphabet inherited from the Phoenicians, the oral tradition of poetry with Homer, and the pottery with its geometric designs.

The Greeks were conscious, on a panhellenic scale, of their common descent, their common language, their common manners and customs, and their common religion. The ideal of unity, however, was incompatible with the isolation of the "city-kingdoms." In 776 B.C. the Olympic games were inaugurated to honor Olympian Zeus, and armistices were declared for their duration. Free Greek citizens from the Greek mainland, the islands, and the colonies competed for the prize, which was an olive branch - the symbol of peace. It was a period of political, economic, and cultural development and a period of colonization as well, although that was an activity which differed substantially from the colonization carried out in later times by European states.

Hellenism continued to waver between the oligarchies, which wanted to hand power to their "select" candidates, and the democrats, who supported a broader and more radical distribution of power. However, they meant a democratic regime that was limited in scope since it still barred women, foreigners, and slaves from participating in the exercise of such power.

At the start of the 5th century the two cities, Athens and Sparta, had joined forces and gained victory over the Persians at Marathon and Salamis. However, from 431 to 404 B.C. they had engaged in the exhausting and catastrophic Peloponnesian War. Thucydides has given us a gripping account of this conflict between Sparta and Athens.

Classical Period - "The Golden Age"

Pericles stamped the Classical Period with the seal of his personality and, despite the horror of war, the flowering of culture in this period was unique in history. The tragedies of Aeschylus, Sophocles, and Euripides; the comedies of Aristophanes; the histories of Herodotus and Thucydides; the unique personality of Socrates; the Parthenon; the sculptures; Pheidias and so many other artists; the wonderful pottery with its red designs - they all constituted a group of people, ideas, creators, and works by which Greece established its eternal fame. Plato and Aristotle pronounced their philosophical systems and sought the revival of the ideal of the "republic" while Isocrates vainly called upon the Greeks to unite. In the 4th century, Philip of Macedon undertook the definitive expulsion of the Persians from lands in the Aegean Sea and rescued the Greeks from enslavement. Philip was succeeded by his twenty-year-old son, Alexander, in 336 B.C.

Alexander the Great

Gifted with physical attributes and intelligence, Alexander was considered the greatest conqueror of the ancient world. Taught by Aristotle and inspired by Greek classical culture, he was also a military genius who mounted an expedition against the Persians. His aspirations were to conquer the Persian empire and to reach the edge of the world and come to the Ocean, which according to Greek belief, surrounded the earth. Within seven years he had conquered the entire Persian state and then decided to conquer India too, which he also succeeded in doing. He died at the age of 33 in 324 B.C. The conquests and achievements of Alexander brought about radical changes in the ancient Greek world, having given access to the wealth of the East.

Hellenistic Period (336-30 B.C.)

Upon the death of Alexander, a bitter struggle broke out among his generals for the succession. The clashes and the quarrels lasted for three centuries as the Macedonian empire was split up among the "successors." Four Kingdoms were formed: the kingdom of Macedonia; the kingdom of Greece proper; the kingdom of Egypt, which was ruled by the dynasty of the Ptolemies, and the kingdom of Antioch, ruled by the dynasty of the Seleucids. Hellenism had now expanded beyond its metropolitan bounds and had created new centers of culture.

The Roman Conquest

But the long-lasting wars among the successors weakened the new states to the extent that they fell easy prey to the Romans. The Romans conquered Greece in 146 B.C., but in conquering the East they were charmed by it and imitated its culture. They were deeply influenced by it in all aspects of their lives, and it changed their habits, manners, and customs. This is why their civilization was known as the "Greco-Roman civilization." The Roman Empire began to decline in the middle of the 4th century A.D.

Byzantine Civilization

In 395 A.D. the Roman Empire was finally dismembered. Its western part fell to the barbarians while the eastern part played an important role in world history for more than a thousand years. With the establishment of Constantinople in 330 A.D. as the capital of the Eastern Roman Empire and the complete predominance of Christianity, the Greeks became conscious of their national identity and laid the foundations of the later powerful Byzantine Empire. Byzantine civilization was considered to be a continuation of ancient Greek civilization with many Roman and Eastern influences. Its main identifying feature was the Christian religion which pervaded its legislation, its literature, its architecture, etc.

In 1096 A.D. the "Frankish" infiltration of the Levant began with the First Crusade. The Crusaders overran the Greek lands. The Fourth Crusade ended with the taking of Constantinople in 1204 and the sharing of the empire among the Crusaders, while Venice imposed itself on the Levant for centuries in parallel with the Turks. Venice dominated some Creek islands either directly or indirectly. Euboea, the Cyclades, the Ionian islands, Crete, and Cyprus were more or less Venetian possessions from 1489 onwards, while in the 15th century, Thasos, Samothrace, Imbros, Lemnos, Chios, Samos, Icaria, and the ports of Ainos in Thrace and Phocaea in Ionia were Genoese dependencies. Rhodes and its neighboring islands had been occupied by the Knights of St. John since 1308.

The dismantling of the Byzantine Empire, however, did not bring about the dismantling of Hellenism. The idea of national unity had already been sufficiently developed to spark the formation of cores of resistance. Michael Palaeologus succeeded in retaking Constantinople in 1262, and the revived empire lived on for another two centuries.

The Fall of Constantinople

Finally, in 1453, Constantinople fell to the Ottoman Turks after a siege of two months. The last emperor of Byzantium, Constantine Palaeologus, fell with the city. Hellenism was then nourished by traditions in which one legend featured very largely: that of the king (Constantine) who had been turned into marble by an angel and hidden from the Turks until the time was ripe for his resurrection and return.

For Hellenism, the Turkish conquest signified catastrophe, decline, and retrogression. Religion played an important role during the first centuries of the conquest in upholding morale and fostering resistance. In the 18th century, however, in parallel with the development of trade in Greek lands, there was a change in economic relations. A Greek urban, middle class began to be formed which, in spite of its peculiar nature, promoted the development of a national conscience.

The Greek War of Independence from the Ottoman Empire began in 1821 and concluded with the winning of independence in 1830. With the support of England, France, and Russia, a monarchy was established. A Bavarian prince, Otto, was named king in 1833. He was deposed 30 years later, and the Great Powers chose a prince of the Danish House of

Glucksberg as his successor. He, George I, became King of the Hellenes.

The World Wars

Greece entered World War I in 1917 on the side of the Allies. After the war, Greece took part in the Allied occupation of Turkey, where many Greeks still lived. In 1921, the Greek army attacked from its base in Smyrna (now Izmir) and marched toward Ankara. The Greeks were defeated by Turkish forces led by Mustafa Kemal (later Ataturk) and were forced to withdraw in the summer of 1922. Smyrna was sacked by the Turks, and more than 1.3 million Greek refugees from Turkey poured into Greece, creating enormous challenges for the Greek economy and society and effectively ending the Megali Idea.

Greece's entry into World War II was precipitated by the Italian invasion on October 28, 1940. That date is celebrated in Greece by the one-word reply—*ochi* ("no")—symbolizing the Greek Prime Minister's rejection of the surrender demanded by Mussolini. Despite Italian superiority in numbers and equipment, determined Greek defenders drove the invaders back into Albania. Hitler was forced to divert German troops to protect his southern flank and attacked Greece in early April 1941. German forces withdrew in October 1944, and the government in exile returned to Athens. After the German withdrawal, the principal Greek resistance movement, which was controlled by the communists, refused to disarm. First the United Kingdom and later the United States gave extensive military and economic aid to the Greek government.

Post World War Greece

Communist successes in 1947-48 enabled them to move freely over much of mainland Greece, but with extensive reorganization and American material support, the Greek National Army was slowly able to regain control over most of the countryside. Yugoslavia closed its borders to the insurgent forces in 1949, after Marshal Tito of Yugoslavia broke with Stalin and the Soviet Union. In August 1949, the National Army under Marshal Alexander Papagos launched a final offensive that forced the remaining insurgents to surrender or flee across the northern border into the territory of Greece's communist neighbors. The insurgency resulted in 100,000 killed and caused catastrophic economic disruption. In addition, at least 25,000 Greeks were either voluntarily or forcibly evacuated to Eastern bloc countries, while 700,000 became displaced persons inside the country. After the 1944-49 Greek civil war, Greece sought to join the Western democracies and became a member of

NATO in 1952. From 1952 to late 1963, Greece was governed by conservative parties - the Greek Rally of Marshal Alexandros Papagos and its successor, the National Radical Union (ERE) of Constantine Karamanlis. In 1963, the Center Union Party of George Papandreou was elected and governed until July 1965. It was followed by a succession of unstable coalition governments.

On April 21, 1967, just before scheduled elections, a group of colonels led by Col. George Papadopoulos seized power in a coup d'etat. Civil liberties were suppressed, special military courts were established, and political parties were dissolved. Several thousand political opponents were imprisoned or exiled to remote Greek islands. In November 1973, following an uprising of students at the Athens Polytechnic University, Gen. Dimitrios Ioannides replaced Papadopoulos and tried to continue the dictatorship.

Gen. Ioannides' attempt in July 1974 to overthrow Archbishop Makarios, the President of Cyprus, brought Greece to the brink of war with Turkey, which invaded Cyprus and occupied part of the island. Senior Greek military officers then withdrew their support from the junta, which toppled. Leading citizens persuaded Karamanlis to return from exile in France to establish a government of national unity until elections could be held. Karamanlis' newly organized party, New Democracy (ND), won elections held in November 1974, and he became prime minister. Following the 1974 referendum which resulted in the rejection of the monarchy, a new constitution was approved by parliament on June 19, 1975, and parliament elected Constantine Tsatsos as President of the republic. In the parliamentary elections of 1977, New Democracy again won a majority of seats. In May 1980, Prime Minister Karamanlis was elected to succeed Tsatsos as president. George Rallis was then chosen party leader and succeeded Karamanlis as Prime Minister.

On January 1, 1981, Greece became the 10th member of the European Community (now the European Union). In parliamentary elections held on October 18, 1981, Greece elected its first socialist government when the Panhellenic Socialist Movement (PASOK), led by Andreas Papandreou, won 172 of 300 seats. On March 29, 1985, after Prime Minister Papandreou declined to support President Karamanlis for a second term, Supreme Court Justice Christos Sartzetakis was elected president by the Greek parliament. Greece had two rounds of parliamentary elections in 1989; both produced weak coalition governments with limited mandates. Party leaders withdrew their support in February 1990, and elections were held on April 8. In the April 1990 election, ND won 150 seats and subsequently gained 2 others.

On January 17, 1996, following a protracted illness, Prime Minister Papandreou resigned and was replaced as Prime Minister by former Minister of Industry Constantine Simitis. In elections held in September 1996, Constantine Simitis was elected Prime Minister. PASOK won 162 seats, New Democracy, 108.

Marine gate, Rhodes

1

Palace of Malia, Crete

Hints on Pronunciation

All the words and phrases are written in a simplified spelling which you read like English. Each letter or combination of letters is used for the sound it usually stands for in English and it ***always*** stands for that sound. Thus, ***oo*** is always pronounced as it is in ***too, boot, tooth, roost,*** never as anything else. Say these words and then pronounce the vowel sound by itself. That is the sound you must use every time you see ***oo*** in the Greek column.

Syllables that are accented, that is, pronounced louder than others, are written in capital letters. In Greek unaccented syllables are not skipped over quickly, as they are in English. ***Curved lines (‿) are used to show sounds that are pronounced together without any break;*** for example, *K‿TEN-ah* meaning "comb," *k‿see-RA-fee* meaning "razor."

Special Points

AY — as in *say*, *may*, *play* but don't drawl it the way we do in English. Example: *HAYR-et-ay* meaning "Hello."

DH — sounds like the *th* in *then*, *this*, *that*. Example: *DHEE-o* meaning "two."

G — sounds something like the sound you make when you gargle. Example: *av-GA* meaning "eggs." However, if you use the *g* in "got" or "gone" you will be understood.

KH — sounds like a very strong *h*. Example: *dhrakh-MEE*, the name of the principal Greek coin. However, the *k* in *king* will be understood.

Harbor front, Chania, Crete

Fira, Santorini

USEFUL WORDS AND PHRASES

GREETINGS AND GENERAL PHRASES

English	*Greek*
Hello *or* **Greetings**	*HA YR-et-ay*

A familiar greeting used somewhat like our "Hi there" or "So long" is:

YA-soo

HAYR-et-ay and *YA-soo* are general expressions of good will and friendliness. They are used both for "Hello" and "Good-by."

Good morning	*ka-lee MA YR-ah*

English	*Greek*
Good evening	*ka-lee SPAYR-ah*
Good night	*ka-lee NEEK-ta*
Sir *or* Mister	*KEE-ree-ay*
Madam	*kee-REE-ah*
Miss	*dhess-pee-NEESS*
How are you?	*TEE KA-net-ay?*
I am well	*EE-may ka-LA*
Excuse me	*seeg-NO-meen*
Please	*pa-ra-ka-LO*
Thank you	*ef-ha-ree-STO*

When someone thanks you, you answer with the word for "please"—*pa-ra-ka-LO*.

Yes	*NAY*
Certainly	*MA-lee-sta*
No	*O-hee*
Do you understand?	*ka-ta-la-VEN-eess?*
I understand	*ka-ta-la-VEN-o*
I don't understand	*DHEN ka-ta-la-VEN-o*
Speak slowly	*MEE-la see-GA*

Fishing village, Monemvasia

English	*Greek*

LOCATION

When you need directions to get somewhere, you can say "Where is it?" and then add the words you need.

Where is it **the restaurant**	*POO EE-nay* *to ess-tee-ah-TO-ree-ohn*
Where is the restaurant?	*POO EE-nay to ess-tee-ah-TO-ree-ohn?*
the hotel	*to k‿sen-o-dho-HEE-ohn*
Where is the hotel?	*POO EE-nay to k‿sen-o-dho-HEE-ohn?*
the railroad station	*o stath-MOHSS*
Where is the railroad station?	*POO EE-nay o stath-MOHSS?*
the toilet	*to MAYR-ohss*
Where is the toilet?	*POO EE-nay to MAYR-ohss?*

English	*Greek*

DIRECTIONS

The answer to your question "Where is such and such?" may be "Turn right" or "Turn left" or "Straight ahead," so you need to know these phrases.

Turn right	*STREEP-say dhek-see-AH*
Turn left	*STREEP-say ah-ree-stay-RA*
Straight ahead	*EE-sa*

It is sometimes useful to say "Please point" or "Show me the way."

Please point	*pa-ra-ka-LO DHEEK-sem-oo*
Show me the way	*DHEEK-sem-oo tohn DHRO-mo*

If you are driving and ask the distance to another town, it will be given you in kilometers, not miles.

Kilometers	*hee-lee-O-met-ra*

One kilometer equals 5/8 of a mile.

NUMBERS

You need to know the numbers.

One	*EN-ah*
Two	*DHEE-o*

English	*Greek*
Three	*TREE-ah*
Four	*TESS-ay-ra*
Five	*PEN-day*
Six	*EK-see*
Seven	*ep-TA*
Eight	*ohk-TO*
Nine	*ay-NAY-ah*
Ten	*DHAY-ka*
Eleven	*EN-dhay-ka*
Twelve	*DHO-dhay-ka*

Notice that the numbers from "thirteen" through "nineteen" are made by saying the word for "ten" and adding the words for "three," "four," etc.

Thirteen	*dhay-ka-TREE-ah*
Fourteen	*dhay-ka-TESS-ay-ra*
Fifteen	*dhay-ka-PEN-day*
Sixteen	*dhay-ka-EK-see*

English	*Greek*
Seventeen	*dhay-ka-ep-TA*
Eighteen	*dhay-ka-ohk-TO*
Nineteen	*dhay-ka-ay-NAY-ah*
Twenty	*EE-ko-see*

For "twenty-one," "twenty-two," etc., use the word for "twenty" followed by the word for "one," "two," etc.

Twenty-one	*EE-ko-see EN-ah*
Twenty-two	*EE-ko-see DHEE-o*
Thirty	*tree-AN-da*
Forty	*sa-RAN-da*
Fifty	*pay-NEEN-da*
Sixty	*ek-SEEN-da*
Seventy	*ev-dho-MEEN-da*
Eighty	*og-DHOHN-da*
Ninety	*en-ay-NEEN-da*
One hundred	*ay-ka-TO*
One thousand	*HEE-lee-ah*

English	*Greek*

WHAT'S THIS?

When you want to know the name of something, you can say "What's this?" and point to the thing you mean.

What is it	*TEE EE-nay*
this	*af-TO*
What's this?	*TEE EE-nay af-TO?*

ASKING FOR THINGS

When you want something, you can say the word for "I want" and add the name of the thing wanted.

I want	*THEL-o*
cigarettes	*see-ga-RAY-ta*
I want cigarettes	*THEL-o see-ga-RAY-ta*
to eat	*na FA-go*
I want to eat	*THEL-o na FA-go*
Give me	*DHOHZ-moo*
Give me matches	*DHOHZ-moo SPEER-ta*

Here are the words for some of the things you may require.

food	*fa-EE*

Inside The Famed Castle, Rhodes

Monemvasia Byzantine Architecture

English	*Greek*
bread	*p‿so-MEE*
butter	*VOO-tee-ro*
soup	*SOO-pa*
water	*nay-RO*
eggs	*av́-GA*
fish	*P‿SA-ree*
meat	*KRAY-ahss*
pork	*hee-ree-NO*
lamb	*ar-NEE*
beef	*vo-dhee-NO*
stew	*en-TRA-dha*
chicken	*KO-ta*
cheese	*tee-REE*
salad	*sa-LA-ta*
vegetables	*la-ha-nee-KA*
potatoes	*pa-TA-tess*
cabbage	*LA-ha-no*
rice	*REE-zee*
chick peas	*ray-VEE-thee-ah*

English	*Greek*
dry beans	*fa-SOHL-ya*
string beans	*fa-soo-LAIK-ya*
peas	*bee-ZEL-ya*
tomatoes	*to-MA-tess*
sugar	*ZA-ha-ree*
salt	*ah-LA-tee*
black pepper	*pee-PAYR-ee*
milk	*GA-la*
curded milk	*ya-GOOR-tee*
ice cream	*pa-go-TO*
fruit	*FROO-ta*
oranges	*por-to-KAL-ya*
lemons	*lay-MOHN-ya*
tobacco	*kap-NOHSS*
wine	*kra-SEE*
a glass of beer	*EN-ah po-TEE-ree BEE-ra*
a cup of coffee	*EN-ah koo-PAI-kee ka-FAY*
a cup of tea	*EN-ah koo-PAI-kee T‿SA-ee*
a general word for anything intoxicating	*p‿yo-TO*

English	*Greek*

MONEY

To find out how much things cost, you say:

How much?	*PO-so?*

TIME

To find out what time it is you say "What hour is it?"

What time is it?	*tee O-ra EE-nay?*

For "two o'clock" you say "it is two."

Two o'clock	*EE-nay DHEE-o*

"Ten past two" is "two and ten."

Ten past two	*DHEE-o kay-DHAY-ka*

"Quarter past five" is "five and a quarter."

Quarter past five	*PEN-day kay TET-ar-to*

Parthenon, Athens

English	*Greek*

"Half past six" is "six and a half."

Half past six	*ek-SEE-mee-see*

"Quarter of eight" is "eight minus a quarter."

Quarter of eight	*ohk-TO pa-ra TET-ar-to*

"Three minutes to nine" is "nine minus three."

Three minutes to nine	*ay-NAY-ah pa-ra TREE-ah*

If you want to know when a movie starts or when a train leaves, you say:

At what time **begins** **the movie**	*tee O-ra* *ar-HEE-zee* *o kee-nee-ma-to-GRA-fohss*
When does the movie start?	*tee O-ra ar-HEE-zee o kee-nee-ma-to-GRA-fohss?*
leaves	*FEV-gee*
the train	*to TREN-o*
When does the train leave?	*tee O-ra FEV-gee to TREN-o?*
Today	*SEE-may-ra*
Tomorrow	*AV-ree-o*
Yesterday	*KH‿THESS*

English	*Greek*

The days of the week are:

Sunday	*kee-ree-ah-KEE*
Monday	*dhef-TAYR-ah*
Tuesday	*TREE-tee*
Wednesday	*tay-TAR-tee*
Thursday	*PEMP-tee*
Friday	*pa-ra-skay-VEE*
Saturday	*SA-va-to*

OTHER USEFUL PHRASES

The following phrases will be useful.

What is your name?	*TEE EE-nay to o-no-MA-soo?*
My name is Peter	*to o-no-MA-moo EE-nay PET-rohss*
How do you say *table* (or anything else) in Greek?	*POHSS LESS* table *ay-lee-nee-KA?*
I am an American	*EE-may ah-may-ree-ka-NOHSS*
I am your friend	*EE-may FEE-lo-soo*

English	*Greek*
Which is the road to Athens?	*P‿YOHSS EE-nay o-DHRO-mohss ya TEEN ah-THEE-na?*
Take me there	*PEE-yay-NEM-ay ay-KEE*
Good-by	*HA YR-et-ay*
So long	*YA-soo*

Tiled Roofs at Monemvasia

ADDITIONAL EXPRESSIONS

English	*Greek*
I am hungry	*pee-NO*
I am thirsty	*dheep-SO*
I am lost	*AY-ha-sa to DHRO-mo*
I am well	*EE-may ka-LA*
Come here!	*ay-LA-tay DHO!*
Right away *or* quickly	*ah-MESS-ohss*
Come quickly!	*ay-LA-tay GREE-go-ra!*
Go quickly!	*pee-YEN-et-ay GREE-go-ra!*
Help!	*vo-EE-thee-ah!*
Help me!	*vo-ee-THEE-sa-TEM-ay!*
Bring help!	*FAYR-et-ay vo-EE-thee-ah!*
I will pay you	*THA sass plee-RO-so*
Where is the town?	*POO EE-nay to hor-YO?*
Where is it?	*POO EE-nay?*

Mouse Island

English	*Greek*
How far is the town?	*PO-so ma-kree-AH EE-nay to hor-YO?*
Is it far?	*EE-nay ma-kree-AH?*
How far is it?	*PO-so ma-kree-AH EE-nay?*
Which way is north?	*ah-PO POO EE-nay o vor-YASS?*
Which is the road to___?	*P‿YOHSS EE-nay o DHRO-mohss ya___?*
Draw me a map	*KA-nay EN-ah HAR-tee*
Take me there	*pee-yay-NEM-ay ay-KEE*
Take me to a doctor	*pee-yay-NEM-ay sto ya-TRO*
Take me to the hospital	*pee-yay-NEM-ay sto no-so-ko-MEE-o*
Danger!	*KEEN-dhee-nohss!*
Gas!	*ah-AYR-ee-ohn!*
Take cover!	*pro-fee-lak-THEE-tay!*
Watch out!	*pro-SEK-sa-tay!*
Wait a minute!	*pay-REE-men-ay mee-AH steeg-MEE!*
Good luck	*sto ka-LO*

FILL-IN SENTENCES

In this section you will find a number of sentences, each containing a blank space which can be filled in with any one of the words in the list that follows. For example, to say "Where can I get some soap?" look for the phrase "Where can I get___?" in the English column and find the Greek expression given beside it: *POO bo-RO na EV-ro___*. Then look for "soap" in the list that follows; the Greek word is *sa-POO-nee*. Put the word for "soap" in the blank space and you get *POO bo-RO na EV-ro sa-POO-nee*.

English	*Greek*
I want___	*THEL-o*
We want___	*THEL-o-may___*
Give me___	*DHOHZ-moo___*
Bring me___	*FA YR-em-oo___*
Where can I get___?	*POO bo-RO na EV-ro___?*
I have___	*A Y-ho___*
We have___	*A Y-ho-may___*
We don't have___	*DHEN A Y-ho-may___*
Have you___?	*A Y-heess___?*

English	*Greek*
	EXAMPLE
I want___ food	*THEL-o* *fa-EE*
I want food	*THEL-o fa-EE*
boiled water	*vraz-MEN-o nay-RO*
hot water	*zess-TO nay-RO*
a cup	*EN-ah koo-PAI-kee*
a fork	*EN-ah pee-ROO-nee*
a glass	*EN-ah po-TEE-ree*
a knife	*EN-ah ma-HAYR-ee*
a plate	*EN-ah pee-AT-o*
a spoon	*EN-ah koo-TA-lee*
a bed	*EN-ah kray-VA-tee*
blankets	*koo-VAYR-tess*
a mosquito net	*MEE-ah koo-noop-YAYR-ah*
a pillow	*EN-ah mak-see-LA-ree*
a room	*EN-ah dho-MA-tee-o*
sheets	*sen-DHO-nee-ah*

English	*Greek*
cigars	*POO-ra*
a pipe	*MEE-ah PEE-pa*
ink	*may-LA-nee*
paper	*har-TEE*
a pen	*MEE-ah PEN-ah*
a pencil	*EN-ah mo-LEE-vee*
a comb	*MEE-ah K‿TEN-ah*
a razor	*EN-ah k‿see-RA-fee*
razor blades	*k‿see-ra-FA-kee-ah*
a shaving brush	*MEE-ah VOORT-sa k‿see-REEZ-ma-tohss*
shaving soap	*sa-POO-nee k‿see-REEZ-ma-tohss*
soap	*sa-POO-nee*
a toothbrush	*MEE-ah o-dhohn-DO-voort-sa*
tooth paste	*o-dhohn-DO pa-sta*
a towel	*MEE-ah pay-SET-ah*
a handkerchief	*EN-ah man-DEE-lee*

English	*Greek*
a raincoat	*EN-ah moo-sa-MA*
a shirt	*EN-ah po-KA-mee-so*
shoe laces	*kor-DHO-nee-ah pa-poots-YOHN*
shoe polish	*vayr-NEE-kee*
shoes	*pa-POOTS-ya*
undershirt	*ay-SO-roo-ha*
undershorts	*SO-vra-ko*
buttons	*koomb-YA*
a needle	*EN-ah vay-LO-nee*
safety pins	*pa-ra-MA-ness*
thread	*klo-STEE*
aspirin	*ah-spee-REE-nee*
a bandage	*EN-ah ay-PEE-dhez-mo*
cotton	*van-VA-kee*
a disinfectant	*EN-ah ah-po-lee-man-tee-KO*
a laxative	*EN-ah ka-THAR-see-o*
gasoline	*ven-ZEE-nee*

Mykonos

Mykonos Main Harbor

English	*Greek*
I want to___	*THEL-o na___*

EXAMPLE

I want to___	*THEL-o na___*
eat	*FA-go*
I want to eat	*THEL-o na FA-go*
be shaved	*k‿see-reess-THO*
buy it	*to ah-go-RA-so*
drink	*pee-O*
have my clothes washed	*PLEE-no ta-ROO-ha-moo*
have my hair cut	*KOHP-so ta mal-YA-moo*
rest	*k‿sek-oo-rass-THO*
sleep	*kee-mee-THO*
take a bath	*PA-ro BAN-yo*
wash up	*plee-THO*
Where is___?	*POO EE-nay___?*

EXAMPLE

Where is___?	*POO EE-nay___?*
a dentist	*EN-ahss o-dhohn-do-ya-TROHSS*

English	*Greek*
Where is a dentist?	*POO EE-nay EN-ahss o-dhohn-do-ya-TROHSS?*
a doctor	*EN-ahss ya-TROHSS*
a mechanic	*EN-ahss mee-ha-nee-KOHSS*
a policeman	*EN-ahss ah-stee-FEE-la-kass*
a porter	*EN-ahss ha-MA-leess*
a servant	*EN-ahss ee-pee-RET-eess*
a shoemaker	*EN-ahss pa-poot-SEESS*
a tailor	*EN-ahss RAP-teess*
a workman	*EN-ahss ayr-GA-teess*
a barber shop	*EN-ah koo-REE-ohn*
a church	*MEE-ah ek-lee-SEE-ah*
a clothing store	*EN-ah em-bo-ree-KO*
a drugstore	*EN-ah far-ma-KEE-o*
filling station	*ga-RAZ*
a garage	*EN-ah ga-RAZ*
a grocery store	*EN-ah ba-KA-lee-ko*
a house	*EN-ah SPEE-tee*

English	*Greek*
a laundry	*EN-ah plin-DEE-ree-o*
a spring (well)	*MEE-ah VREE-see*
the bridge	*ee YEF-ee-ra*
the bus	*to lay-o-fo-REE-o*
the camp	*to stra-TO-pedh-o*
the city	*ee PO-leess*
the highway	*o dhee-MO-see-ohss DHRO-mohss*
the hospital	*to no-so-ko-MEE-o*
the market	*ee ah-go-RA*
the nearest town	*to plee-see-ESS-tay-ro hor-YO*
the police station	*ee ah-stee-no-MEE-ah*
the post office	*to ta-hee-dhro-MEE-o*
the railroad	*o see-dhee-RO-dhro-mohss*
the river	*to po-TA-mee*
the road	*o DHRO-mohss*
the street car	*to TRAM*
the telegraph office	*to tee-leg-ra-FEE-o*
the telephone	*to tee-LEF-o-no*
the town	*to hor-YO*

English	*Greek*
I am___	*EE-may___*
He is___	*EE-nay___*

EXAMPLE

I am___ an American	*EE-may___ ah-may-ree-ka-NOHSS*
I am an American	*EE-may ah-may-ree-ka-NOHSS*
sick	*AR-o-stohss*
tired	*koo-raz-MEN-ohss*
wounded	*trav-ma-TEE-ahss*
We are___	*EE-ma-stay___*
You are___	*EE-sthay___*
They are___	*EE-nay___*
Are you___?	*EE-sthay___?*

EXAMPLE

We are— Americans	*EE-ma-stay___ ah-may-ree-ka-NEE*
We are Americans	*EE-ma-stay ah-may-ree-ka-NEE*
sick	*AR-o-stee*
tired	*koo-raz-MEN-ee*
wounded	*trav-ma-TEE-ay*

English	*Greek*
Is it___?	*EE-nay___?*
It is___	*EE-nay___*
It is not___	*DHEN EE-nay___*
This is___	*af-TO EE-nay___*
That is___	*ay-KEE-no EE-nay___*
It is too___	*EE-nay PA-ra po-LEE___*
It is very___	*EE-nay po-LEE___*

EXAMPLE

It is not___	*DHEN EE-nay___*
cold	*KREE-o*
It is not cold	*DHEN EE-nay KREE-o*
clean	*ka-tha-RO*
dirty	*ah-KA-thar-to*
cold	*KREE-o*
hot *or* warm	*zess-TO*
cheap	*ef-thee-NO*
expensive	*ah-kree-VO*
large	*may-GA-lo*
small	*mee-KRO*

English	*Greek*
bad	*ka-KO*
good	*ka-LO*
enough	*ar-kay-TO*
much	*po-LEE*

Acropolis, Athens

IMPORTANT SIGNS

Greek	*English*
ΣΤΑΣΙΣ	Stop
ΒΡΑΔΥΠΟΡΕΙΑ	Go slow
ΚΙΝΔΥΝΟΣ	Danger!
ΔΕΞΙΑ	Keep to the Right
ΔΗΜΟΣΙΑ ΕΡΓΑ	Road under Construction
ΕΠΙΚΙΝΔΥΝΟΣ ΚΑΜΡΗ	Dangerous Curve
ΚΙΝΔΥΝΟΣ	Dangerous Crossing
ΔΙΑΣΤΑΥΡΩΣΙΣ	Intersection
ΑΠΑΓΟΡΕΥΕΤΑΙ Η ΣΤΑΘΜΕΥΣΙΣ	No Parking
ΑΠΑΓΟΡΕΥΕΤΑΙ Η ΕΙΣΟΔΟΣ	No Admittance
ΓΥΝΑΙΚΕΣ	Women
ΑΝΔΡΕΣ	Men.
ΑΠΑΓΟΡΕΥΕΤΑΙ ΤΟ ΚΑΠΝΙ-ΣΜΑ	No Smoking
ΑΠΑΓΟΡΕΥΕΤΑΙ ΤΟ ΠΤΥΕΙΝ	No Spitting
ΕΙΣΟΔΟΣ	Entrance
ΕΞΟΔΟΣ	Exit

Mykonos

ALPHABETICAL WORD LIST

English	*Greek*
	A
a	*EN-ah* ***or*** *MEE-ah* ***or*** *EN-ahss*
am	
I am___	*EE-may___*
Americans	*ah-may-ree-ka-NEE*
American soldiers	*ah-may-ree-ka-NEE stra-tee-O-tess*
I am an American	*EE-may ah-may-ree-ka-NOHSS*
and	*kay*
are	
Are you___?	*EE-sthay___?*
They are___	*EE-nay___*
We are___	*EE-ma-stay___*
aspirin	*ah-spee-REE-nee*

English	*Greek*
	B
bad	*ka-KO*
bandage	*ay-PEE-dhez-mo*
barber shop	*koo-REE-ohn*
bath	
I want to take a bath	*THEL-o na PA-ro BAN-yo*
beans	
dry beans	*fa-SOHL-ya*
string beans	*fa-soo-LAIK-ya*
bed	*kray-VA-tee*
beef	*vo-dhee-NO*
beer	*BEE-ra*
a glass of beer	*EN-ah po-TEE-ree BEE-ra*
begins	*ar-HEE-zee*
black pepper	*pee-PAYR-ee*
blankets	*koo-VAYR-tess*
boiled water	*vraz-MEN-o nay-RO*
bread	*p‿so-MEE*
bridge	*YEF-ee-ra*

English	Greek
bring	
Bring help!	*FAYR-et-ay vo-EE-thee-ah!*
Bring me___	*FAYR-em-oo___*
brush	*VOORT-sa*
shaving brush	*VOORT-sa k‿see-REEZ-ma-tohss*
bus	*lay-o-fo-REE-o*
butter	*VOO-tee-ro*
buttons	*koomb-YA*
buy	
I want to buy it	*THEL-o na to ah-go-RA-so*

C

cabbage	*LA-ha-no*
camp	*stra-TO-pedh-o*
certainly	*MA-lee-sta*
cheap	*ef-thee-NO*
cheese	*tee-REE*
chicken	*KO-ta*
chick peas	*ray-VEE-thee-ah*

English	*Greek*
church	*ek-lee-SEE-ah*
cigarettes	*see-ga-RAY-ta*
cigars	*POO-ra*
city	*PO-leess*
clean	*ka-tha-RO*
clothing store	*em-bo-ree-KO*
coffee	*ka-FAY*
a cup of coffee	*EN-ah koo-PAI-kee ka-FAY*
cold	*KREE-o*
comb	*K‿TEN-ah*
come	
Come here!	*ay-LA-tay ay-DHO!*
Come quickly!	*ay-LA-tay GREE-go-ra!*
cotton	*van-VA-kee*
cover	
Take cover!	*pro-fee-lak-THEE-tay!*
cup	*koo-PAI-kee*
a cup of___	*EN-ah koo-PAI-kee___*
curded milk	*ya-GOOR-tee*

Velissaropoulos Mansion interior, Syros

View Of Town, Corfu

English	Greek
	D
Danger!	*KEEN-dhee-nohss!*
dentist	*o-dhohn-do-ya-TROHSS*
dirty	*ah-KA-thar-to*
disinfectant	*ah-po-lee-man-tee-KO*
doctor	*ya-TROHSS*
Take me to a doctor	*pee-yay-NEM-ay sto ya-TRO*
drachmas	*dhrakh-MESS*
Draw me a map	*KA-nay EN-ah HAR-tee*
drink	
I want to drink	*THEL-o na pee-O*
intoxicating drink	*p‿yo-TO*
drugstore	*far-ma-KEE-o*
dry beans	*fa-SOHL-ya*
	E
eat	
I want to eat	*THEL-o na FA-go*
eggs	*av-GA*
eight	*ohk-TO*

English	*Greek*
eighteen	*dhay-ka-ohk-TO*
eighty	*og-DHOHN-da*
eleven	*EN-dhay-ka*
enough	*ar-kay-TO*
Excuse me	*seeg-NO-meen*
evening	
Good evening	*ka-lee SPAYR-ah*
expensive	*ah-kree-VO*

F

far	*ma-kree-AH*
Is it far?	*EE-nay ma-kree-AH?*
How far is it?	*PO-so ma-kree-AH EE-nay?*
fifteen	*dhay-ka-PEN-day*
fifty	*pay-NEEN-da*
filling station	*ga-RAZ*
fish	*P‿SA-ree*
five	*PEN-day*
food	*fa-EE*
fork	*pee-ROO-nee*

English	*Greek*
forty	*sa-RAN-da*
four	*TESS-ay-ra*
fourteen	*dhay-ka-TESS-ay-ra*
Friday	*pa-ra-skay-VEE*
friend	
I am your friend	*EE-may FEE-lo-soo*
fruit	*FROO-ta*

G

garage	*ga-RAZ*
Gas!	*ah-AYR-ee-ohn!*
gasoline	*ven-ZEE-nee*
get	
Where can I get___?	*POO bo-RO na EV-ro___?*
Give me___	*DHOHZ-moo___*
glass	*po-TEE-ree*
a glass of___	*EN-ah po-TEE-ree___*
go	
Go quickly!	*pee-YEN-et-ay GREE-go-ra!*

English	*Greek*
good	*ka-LO*
Good evening	*ka-lee SPAYR-ah*
Good luck	*sto ka-LO*
Good morning	*ka-lee MAYR-ah*
Good night	*ka-lee NEEK-ta*
Good-by	*YA-soo* **or** *HAYR-et-ay*
Greetings *or* Hello	*YA-soo* **or** *HAYR-et-ay*
grocery store	*ba-KA-lee-ko*

H

hair	
I want to have my hair cut	*THEL-o na KOHP-so ta mal-YA-moo*
Halt!	*sta-THEE-tay!*
handkerchief	*man-DEE-lee*
have	
Have you___?	*AY-heess___?*
I have___	*AY-ho___*
I don't have___	*DHEN AY-ho___*

English	*Greek*
We have___	*AY-ho-may___*
We don't have___	*DHEN AY-ho-may___*
he	
He is___	*EE-nay___*
Hello	*HAYR-et-ay*
Help!	*vo-EE-thee-ah!*
Bring help!	*FAYR-et-ay vo-EE-thee-ah!*
Help me!	*vo-ee-THEE-sa-TEM-ay!*
here	*ay-DHO*
Come here!	*ay-LA-tay DHO!*
highway	*dhee-MO-see-ohss DHRO-mohss*
hospital	*no-so-ko-MEE-o*
Take me to the hospital	*pee-yay-NEM-ay sto no-so-ko-MEE-o*
hot *or* **warm**	*zess-TO*
hot water	*zess-TO nay-RO*
hotel	*k‿sen-o-dho-HEE-ohn*
Where is the hotel?	*POO EE-nay to k‿sen-o-dho-HEE-ohn?*
house	*SPEE-tee*

Delphi

English	*Greek*
how	
How are you?	*TEE KA-net-ay?*
How do you say *table* in Greek?	*POHSS LESS* table *ay-lee-nee-KA?*
How far is it?	*PO-so ma-kree-AH EE-nay?*
How much?	*PO-so?*
hundred	*ay-ka-TO*
hungry	
I am hungry	*pee-NO*

English	*Greek*
	I
I	
I am___	*EE-may___*
I have___	*AY-ho___*
I don't have___	*DHEN AY-ho___*
I want___	*THEL-o___*
I want to___	*THEL-o na___*
ice cream	*pa-go-TO*
in Greek	*ay-lee-nee-KA*
ink	*may-LA-nee*
is	
It is___	*EE-nay___*
Is it___?	*EE-nay___?*
It is not___	*DHEN EE-nay___*
It is too___	*EE-nay PA-ra po-LEE___*
It is very___	*EE-nay po-LEE___*
	K
kilometers	*hee-lee-O-met-ra*
knife	*ma-HAYR-ee*

English	*Greek*
	L
lamb	*ar-NEE*
large	*may-GA-lo*
laundry	*plin-DEE-ree-o*
laxative	*ka-THAR-see-o*
leaves	*FEV-gee*
When does the train leave?	*tee O-ra FEV-gee to TREN-o?*
left	
Turn left	*STREEP-say ah-ree-stay-RA*
lemons	*lay-MOHN-ya*
lost	
I am lost	*AY-ha-sa to DHRO-mo*
luck	
Good luck	*sto ka-LO*
	M
Madam	*kee-REE-ah*
map	*HAR-tee*
Draw me a map	*KA-nay EN-ah HAR-tee*

English	*Greek*
market	*ah-go-RA*
matches	*SPEER-ta*
meat	*KRAY-ahss*
mechanic	*mee-ha-nee-KOHSS*
milk	*GA-la*
curded milk	*ya-GOOR-tee*
Miss	*dhess-pee-NEESS*
Mister	*KEE-ree-ay*
Monday	*dhef-TAYR-ah*
morning	
Good morning	*ka-lee MAYR-ah*
mosquito net	*koo-noop-YAYR-ah*
movie	*kee-nee-ma-to-GRA-fohss*
When does the movie start?	*tee O-ra ar-HEE-zee o kee-nee-ma-to-GRA-fohss?*
much	*po-LEE*

N

name	
My name is___	*to o-no-MA-moo EE-nay___*
What is your name?	*TEE EE-nay to o-no-MA-soo?*

English	*Greek*
near	*kohn-DA*
the nearest town	*plee-see-ESS-tay-ro hor-YO*
needle	*vay-LO-nee*
nine	*ay-NA Y-ah*
nineteen	*dhay-ka-ay-NA Y-ah*
ninety	*en-ay-NEEN-da*
no	*O-hee*
north	*vor-YASS*
Which way is north?	*ah-PO POO EE-nay o vor-YASS?*

Mykonos' Famed Windmills

English	*Greek*
	O
one	*EN-ah*
oranges	*por-to-KAL-ya*
	P
paper	*har-TEE*
pay	
I will pay you	*THA sass plee-RO-so*
peas	*bee-ZEL-ya*
chick peas	*ray-VEE-thee-ah*
pen	*PEN-ah*
pencil	*mo-LEE-vee*
pepper	
black pepper	*pee-PAYR-ee*
pillow	*mak-see-LA-ree*
pins	
safety pins	*pa-ra-MA-ness*
pipe	*PEE-pa*

English	*Greek*
plate	*pee-AT-o*
please	*pa-ra-ka-LO*
point	
Please point	*pa-ra-ka-LO DHEEK-sem-oo*
policeman	*ah-stee-FEE-la-kass*
police station	*ah-stee-no-MEE-ah*
pork	*hee-ree-NO*
porter	*ha-MA-leess*
post office	*ta-hee-dhro-MEE-o*
potatoes	*pa-TA-tess*

Q

Quickly!	*GREE-go-ra!*
Come quickly!	*ay-LA-tay GREE-go-ra!*
Go quickly!	*pee-YEN-et-ay GREE-go-ra!*

R

railroad	*see-dhee-RO-dhro-mohss*
railroad station	*stath-MOHSS*
Where is the railroad station?	*POO EE-nay o stath-MOHSS?*

Knossos Palace, Crete

Riding Donkeys to the Acropolis

English	*Greek*
raincoat	*moo-sa-MA*
razor	*k‿see-RA-fee*
razor blades	*k‿see-ra-FA-kee-ah*
rest	
I want to rest	*THEL-o na k‿sek-oo-rass-THO*
restaurant	*ess-tee-ah-TO-ree-ohn*
Where is the restaurant?	*POO EE-nay to ess-tee-ah-TO-ree-ohn?*
rice	*REE-zee*
right	
Right away	*ah-MESS-ohss*
Turn right	*STREEP-say dhek-see-AH*
river	*po-TA-mee*
road	*DHRO-mohss*
Which is the road to___?	*P‿YOHSS EE-nay o-DHRO-mohss ya___?*
room	*dho-MA-tee-o*

English	*Greek*
	S
safety pins	*pa-ra-MA-ness*
salad	*sa-LA-ta*
salt	*ah-LA-tee*
Saturday	*SA-va-to*
say	
How do you say *table* in Greek?	*POHSS LESS* table *ay-lee-nee-KA?*
servant	*ee-pee-RET-eess*
seven	*ep-TA*
seventeen	*dhay-ka-ep-TA*
seventy	*ev-dho-MEEN-da*
shave	
I want to be shaved	*THEL-o na k‿see-reess-THO*
shaving brush	*VOORT-sa k‿see-REEZ-ma-tohss*
shaving soap	*sa-POO-nee k‿see-REEZ-ma-tohss*
sheets	*sen-DHO-nee-ah*
shirt	*po-KA-mee-so*

English	*Greek*
shoes	*pa-POOTS-ya*
shoe laces	*kor-DHO-nee-ah pa-poots-YOHN*
shoe polish	*vayr-NEE-kee*
shoemaker	*pa-poot-SEESS*
show	
Show me the way	*DHEEK-sem-oo tohn DHRO-mo*
sick	
I am sick	*EE-may AR-o-stohss*
We are sick	*EE-ma-stay AR-o-stee*
Sir	*KEE-ree-ay*
six	*EK-see*
sixteen	*dhay-ka-EK-see*
sixty	*ek-SEEN-da*
sleep	*kee-mee-THO*
I want to sleep	*THEL-o na kee-mee-THO*
slowly	
Speak slowly	*MEE-la see-GA*
small	*mee-KRO*
soap	*sa-POO-nee*
shaving soap	*sa-POO-nee k‿see-REESS-ma-tohss*

Erectheum, Acropolis, Athens

English	*Greek*
So long	*YA-soo*
soup	*SOO-pa*

English	*Greek*
speak	
Speak slowly	*MEE-la see-GA*
spoon	*koo-TA-lee*
spring (well)	*VREE-see*
start	
When does the movie start?	*tee O-ra ar-HEE-zee o kee-nee-ma-to-GRA-fohss?*
station	
police station	*ah-stee-no-MEE-ah*
railroad station	*stath-MOHSS*
stew	*en-TRA-dha*
store	
clothing store	*em-bo-ree-KO*
grocery store	*ba-KA-lee-ko*
Straight ahead	*EE-sa*
street car	*TRAM*
sugar	*ZA-ha-ree*
Sunday	*kee-ree-ah-KEE*

English	*Greek*
	T
tailor	*RAP-teess*
take	
Take cover!	*pro-fee-lak-THEE-tay!*
Take me to a doctor	*pee-yay-NEM-ay sto ya-TRO*
Take me to the hospital	*pee-yay-NEM-ay sto no-so-ko-MEE-o*
Take me there	*pee-yay-NEM-ay ay-KEE*
tea	*T‿SA-ee*
a cup of tea	*EN-ah koo-PAI-kee T‿SA-ee*
telegraph office	*tee-leg-ra-FEE-o*
telephone	*tee-LEF-o-no*
ten	*DHAY-ka*
Thank you	*ef-ha-ree-STO*
That is___	*ay-KEE-no EE-nay—*
the	*o* or *ee* or *to*
there	*ay-KEE*
Take me there	*pee-yay-NEM-ay ay-KEE*
they	
They are___	*EE-nay___*

English	*Greek*
thirsty	
I am thirsty	*dheep-SO*
thirteen	*dhay-ka-TREE-ah*
thirty	*tree-AN-da*
this	*af-TO*
This is___	*af-TO EE-nay—*
What's this?	*TEE EE-nay af-TO?*
thousand	*HEE-lee-ah*
thread	*klo-STEE*
three	*TREE-ah*
Thursday	*PEMP-tee*
time	
At what time?	*tee O-ra?*
What time is it?	*tee O-ra EE-nay?*
tired	
I am tired	*EE-may koo-raz-MEN-ohss*
We are tired	*EE-ma-stay koo-raz-MEN-ee*
tobacco	*kap-NOHSS*
today	*SEE-may-ra*

English	*Greek*
toilet	*MAYR-ohss*
Where's the toilet?	*POO EE-nay to MAYR-ohss?*
tomatoes	*to-MA-tess*
tomorrow	*AV-ree-o*
too much	*PA-ra po-LEE*
toothbrush	*o-dhohn-DO-voort-sa*
tooth paste	*o-dhohn-DO pa-sta*
towel	*pay-SET-ah*
town	*hor-YO*
Where is the town?	*POO EE-nay to hor-YO?*
How far is the town?	*PO-so ma-kree-AH EE-nay to hor-YO?*
the nearest town	*to plee-see-ESS-tay-ro hor-YO*
train	*TREN-o*
When does the train leave?	*tee O-ra FEV-gee to TREN-o?*
Tuesday	*TREE-tee*
turn	
Turn right	*STREEP-say dhek-see-AH*
Turn left	*STREEP-say ah-ree-stay-RA*

English	*Greek*
twelve	*DHO-dhay-ka*
twenty	*EE-ko-see*
twenty-one	*EE-ko-see EN-ah*
twenty-two	*EE-ko-see DHEE-o*
two	*DHEE-o*

The Fortress Entrance, Corfu

English	*Greek*
	U
understand	
Do you understand?	*ka-ta-la-VEN-eess?*
I understand	*ka-ta-la-VEN-o*
I don't understand	*DHEN ka-ta-la-VEN-o*
undershirt	*ay-SO-roo-ha*
undershorts	*SO-vra-ko*
	V
vegetables	*la-ha-nee-KA*
	W
wait	
Wait a minute	*pay-REE-men-ay mee-AH steeg-MEE*
want	
I want___	*THEL-o___*
I want to___	*THEL-o na___*
warm *or* hot	*zess-TO*

English	*Greek*
wash up	
I want to wash up	*THEL-o na plee-THO*
I want to have my clothes washed	*THEL-o na PLEE-no ta-ROO-ha-moo*
Watch out!	*pro-SEK-sa-tay*
water	*nay-RO*
boiled water	*vraz-MEN-o nay-RO*
hot water	*zess-TO nay-RO*
way	
Show me the way	*DHEEK-sem-oo tohn DHRO-mo*
we	
We are___	*EE-ma-stay___*
We want___	*THEL-o may___*
Wednesday	*tay-TAR-tee*
well	
I am well	*EE-may ka-LA*
welcome	
You're welcome	*pa-ra-ka-LO*

English	*Greek*
what	
What is it?	*TEE EE-nay?*
What is your name?	*TEE EE-nay to o-no-MA-soo?*
when	
When does the movie start?	*tee O-ra ar-HEE-zee o kee-nee-ma-to-GRA-fohss?*
When does the train leave?	*tee O-ra FEV-gee to TREN-o?*
where	
Where is it?	*POO EE-nay?*
which	
Which way is north?	*ah-PO POO EE-nay o vor-YASS?*
Which is the road to___?	*P‿YOHSS EE-nay o DHRO-mohss ya___?*
wine	*kra-SEE*
workman	*ayr-GA-teess*
wounded	
I am wounded	*EE-may trav-ma-TEE-ahss*
We are wounded	*EE-ma-stay trav-ma-TEE-ay*

English	*Greek*
	Y
yes	*NAY*
yesterday	*KH‿THESS*
you	
I will pay you	*THA say plee-RO-so*
Have you___?	*AY-heess___?*
You are___	*EE-sthay___*
Are you___?	*EE-sthay___?*

Entry to Acropolis, the High Place, Athens

Old Town, Corfu